Early Childhood Curriculum

An Easy-to-Follow Guide for Caregivers
of Babies Ages 0–12 Months

by Betty Sue Hanks

AuthorHouse™
1663 Liberty Drive
Bloomington, IN 47403
www.authorhouse.com
Phone: 1-800-839-8640

First published by AuthorHouse 10/25/2011

ISBN: 978-1-4520-6374-4 (sc)
ISBN: 978-1-4520-6478-9 (ebk)

Printed in the United States of America

This book is printed on acid-free paper.

Early Childhood Curriculum

An Easy-to-Follow Guide for Caregivers
of Babies Ages 0–12 Months

by Betty Sue Hanks

About the Author

Betty Sue Hanks is a native Texan and the eleventh of thirteen children. She has been in Bryan, Texas for much of her life; she and her late husband Melvin have five children, sons Melvin and Derrick, and three daughters, RoShunda, Tanisha and Tashara.

Hanks received her Bachelor of Science degree from Prairie View A&M in 1965, and her Master of Education Degree from Texas A&M in 1969. She has also participated in graduate courses at Texas A&M.

In addition to being a student, Hanks has also been a teacher at many levels. She was a teacher for the Bryan ISD for thirty years, and during that time she supervised and was a tutor for student teachers, was a GED advisor, and made many educational presentations to different audiences. She has been involved in a number of organizations; the Girl Scouts, Texas Education Agency, Bethune Woman's Club, City Mission, Prenatal Clinic, Alpha Kappa Alpha Sorority, and the Children's Museum of the Brazos Valley, just to name a few. Hanks also established scholarships for two high school students, and a similar program exists for her employees as well.

Another of Hanks' achievements is the Big Top Learning Center. She has been the owner and director of the center for 28 years, and it is a nationally accredited center. This means that Hanks and her staff went through the voluntary process of becoming accredited through the National Association for the Education of Young Children to demonstrate that their program met the national standards of excellence. In addition to providing excellent child care and education to its patrons, the center also is a place for college students majoring in this area to come and learn about their field.

The Mayor of Bryan declared March 6 as *"Big Top Learning Center Day"* for the accomplishments of the center. In 2001 Hanks was named *"Administrator of the Year of the Brazos Valley Association for the Education of Young Children,"* and she is listed in the 2002 *"Who's Who National Register"* as an Honored Professional for Executives and Business. Hanks is also a validator for the National Association for the Education of Young Children.

Dedication

Dedicated to
my daughters,
RoShunda,
Tanisha,
and
Tashara Hanks
and my sons,
Melvin Jr. and Derrick Hanks

Acknowledgements

This curriculum is a result of many trials and errors, ideas from readings, teachers, parents, volunteers, classes, workshops, observations, and assessments of classrooms throughout the country over the past 28 years.

Many thanks go to the teachers, teacher assistants and clerks of Big Top Learning Center for their input and support.

Special thanks to Dimple Suseberry, Tanisha, Tashara and RoShunda Hanks for helping me arrange the material in order.

In addition, extra appreciation to the Brazos Valley Workforce Development Board–Child Care Management Services for their support, trainings and workshops they offered; Dr. Margarita Gangotena, faculty member, Blinn College, Bryan, Texas for her encouragement, and looking over the curriculum; Dr. Mary Nichter, Assistant Professor of Counselor Education at Sam Houston State University for having her Blinn College Child Development class critique the curriculum; Dr. Maggie McGuire, Associate Professor at Texas A&M University, Corpus Christi, Texas for her input and encouragement; and Adilia Frazer, Children Niños Bilingual Education Trainer and Consultant for her input and encouragement.

Much recognition goes to the many Mother Goose and traditional nursery rhymes, and to the stories and finger plays, for which no author has been found.

The author wishes to acknowledge with great gratitude, the patience and encouragement of late husband, Melvin Hanks Sr., and daughters, RoShunda, Tanisha and Tashara Hanks.

Early Childhood Curriculum

The *Early Childhood Curriculum* book consists of sequential developmental skills and activities. Each age group (0-6 months) and (6-12 months) contains a theme with different activities for the infant, and the units follow these themes. This curriculum is arranged and organized to ensure that cognitive, physical, emotional, language and social areas are addressed. Activities are developmentally appropriate, so that the children can receive the best possible stimulation. This book contains lessons, ideas, and activities that any person would be able to use. People, including parents, presenters, school administrators, graduate students, staff members in childcare laboratories, and early childhood teachers, are all individuals that could benefit from using this curriculum.

This curriculum contains units and ideas that are simple and easy to understand, so that readers, parents and teachers, can use it on a daily basis, both in the classroom and at home. It is functional and pleasing to the eye, and it covers quality, not just quantity. This curriculum is also unique because it is user friendly. The simplicity is convenient for our readers' and professionals' busy schedules. Parents and professionals rarely have the time or luxury of uninterrupted periods to sit, read, and search through and pull out the information that is needed. This simplified version gives them that opportunity.

The latest research shows that between birth to three years of age is the time when a child's mental capacity is the greatest. Research illustrates that if positive and appropriate stimulation of a child's mind is provided, the child will become a better-rounded individual. Recent research also supports the link between literacy and school success; literacy refers to reading and writing skills, and building oral language skills, such as listening and speaking. Childcare providers can foster the development of literacy in children. Strategies used to develop reading and writing include: listening to stories, reading stories, talking and listening to children, playing sound games, saying nursery rhymes, singing songs, singing and saying words that rhyme, using phonetic sounds, exploring rhythms, scribbling, and verbally labeling objects and events. Caregivers and parents can use seasonal songs, rhymes and stories throughout the year. Also, choose and use age appropriate toys, songs, rhymes, and books that go along with the themes and units in the curriculum. The appropriate books to use with infants are board books and plastic books with real photos that can be seen easily.

"The Early Childhood Curriculum Resource Book" by Betty Hanks is available.

Introduction

Caring for infants is primarily about trust, building relationships and making the most out of everyday experiences. The latest research says the first three years of life are more critical to a child's development than we ever imagined. According to studies, more rapid brain development takes place during these years than at any other time of life. Children's brains are being wired into patterns for emotional, social, physical and cognitive development.

Children are naturally curious, and this curiosity provides motivation, which enables them to discover their environment. Interaction between the caregiver and the baby will include a variety of activities, songs, rhymes, and toys. Recent research indicates that reading to young children from six months to three years of age dramatically increases early literacy skills. Reading aloud to children helps develop neural connections for language processing. In addition, babies are not developmentally capable of using problem solving skills; they are mainly told what you want them to see, hear and do. The activities here consist of talking to babies, telling them what you want them to do, what they are doing and what they see. With the babies that are talking or "babbling", let the infant dominate the conversation. The caregiver or parent should listen attentively and respond when appropriate. The most important component is that the caregiver reads and talks constantly to the babies, telling them what they and other babies are doing, seeing, smelling, feeling, tasting and hearing. Also, caregivers should act out the songs, rhymes, activities and finger plays, and sing to babies about everything. Talking and singing to babies produces endorphins that stimulate the brain. When the brain is stimulated, babies are more receptive to learning. Talk to babies in different voice tones, such as soft and loud, high and low, calm and excited. The more you talk, the more they learn. While babies are playing and being taken care of, talk to them about the shape, size, color and texture of objects. Also, use sign language to communicate with babies. Research by Joseph Garcia states that babies can express thoughts long before they understand language, and sign language has been proven to promote literacy development.

When practical, let the older babies do the activity with the caregiver or parent's guidance and assistance. In addition, the activities should be done repetitively. While doing the activities babies may sit in a soft play area, on the caregiver or parent's lap, lay on a play mat, or sit on the floor. Activities may also be done when changing diapers, when the baby is being fed or when the baby is being held.

Always continue to talk and sing to the infants; sing to them about everything. Songs can be familiar tunes with made up words or they can be an actual song. No matter what the activity is, it can be referred to in a song.

For example, the teacher could sing the following words to the tune of *"Row, Row, Row Your Boat":*

> *"Let's have fun with the mobiles, fun with the mobiles.*
> *Look at them turn around and around.*
> *Let's look at them turn around and then stop, stop."*

Singing is important because the latest research shows that from birth to three years of age a child's mental capacity is the greatest. Research illustrates that if positive and appropriate stimulation of a child's mind is provided, the child will become a more well-rounded individual.

This curriculum reflects progressive thinking. It offers fresh insight and makes provisions for the best materials and activities to the childcare professional or parent in order (for them) to improve the quality of childcare for all children.

NOTE: The songs and nursery rhymes in this curriculum may be found in the *Piggy Back Song Book, Finger Frolics,* the *Every Day in Every Way Resource Book,* and in *The Early Childhood Curriculum Resource Guide.* If you do not have access to a suggested song or rhyme, it is perfectly fine to substitute your own that is appropriate for the theme.

Table of Contents

Table of Contents *(Continued)*

Reminder to Readers

All activities in this curriculum should be supervised and age appropriate.

Always use Health and Safety Practices.

AS YOU DO THE ACTIVITIES IN THIS CURRICULUM, PAY SPECIAL ATTENTION TO THE FOLLOWING ICONS AND THEIR MEANINGS:

	REMEMBER TO MAKE EYE CONTACT WITH AND SMILE AT THE BABY
	NEVER LEAVE THE BABY UNATTENDED AND USE EXTRA PRECAUTION AND CARE DURING THESE ACTIVITIES
	WASH YOURS AND THE BABY'S HANDS AND SANITIZE ITEMS
	ENTHUSIASTICALLY ENCOURAGE THE BABY IN HER EFFORTS
	SONGS, RHYMES, AND MUSICAL ACTIVITIES

The World Around Me

T H E M E I

LOOK, LOOK, LOOK

INFANTS 0 – 6 MONTHS

LARGE MOTOR SKILLS

Place the baby in a different direction in the crib each day so she can look at the things hanging over her head. Talk to the baby about what is hanging. Put her on her back on a mat and swing a toy from side to side. Talk about what the baby sees and what you are doing. See if she turns to look at the objects.

SMALL MOTOR SKILLS

Place the baby in a different direction each day in the crib so she can look at things in the environment. Tell the baby what she is looking at. Give her a soft, small toy to look at, grasp and squeeze. Talk about what she is doing.

SENSORY PERCEPTION

Hang colorful swatches of fabric on a mobile across the crib so that the baby can see them. Tell the baby what she is looking at and talk about colors and textures.

LANGUAGE SKILLS

Hold up some interesting objects for the baby to see. See if she will follow the objects with her eyes. Tell the baby what she is looking at.

SOCIAL AND EMOTIONAL

When the parent comes in and the baby sees the parent, notice the baby's reaction and say, "There's daddy/mommy."

LARGE MOTOR SKILLS

Gently swing a toy in front of the baby and encourage the baby to look at the toy and catch it. Then say, "See the toy." "Catch the toy." "Push." or "Bat the toy."

SMALL MOTOR SKILLS

Help the baby drop a peg or toy onto the mat. Encourage the baby to watch the caregiver pick it up. Encourage the baby to pick up the toy. Repeat this action and increase difficulty by using a container or basket for the baby to reach into.

SENSORY PERCEPTION

Play the "Following Moving Objects" game. This game consists of an object moved back and forth for the baby's eyes to follow. Swing a hanging object back and forth. Encourage the baby to look where the object goes.

LANGUAGE SKILLS

Read: *"What Does Baby See?"* by Denise Lewis Patrick.

SOCIAL EMOTIONAL

Arrange baby and family pictures inside the crib for the baby to look at and talk about. Make a peek-a-boo book with various pictures, including the baby and her family, hiding under fabric swatches. Notice the baby's expression when you or the baby uncover the picture.

MIRRORING FUN

INFANTS 0- 6 MONTHS

LARGE MOTOR SKILLS

Place the baby on her tummy in front of a mirror. Tap your fingers on the left side and then the right side of the mirror to get the baby's attention, and see if the baby moves from side to side. Talk to the baby about what she sees in the mirror.

SMALL MOTOR SKILLS

While looking in the mirror, touch the baby's nose with her own hand and say, "Here's your nose;" then repeat for her head, eyes, and ears. Remember to wash your hands before and after this type of activity.

SENSORY PERCEPTION

Looking in a mirror with the baby, make a funny face. Say to the baby, "Look at my funny face." Observe the baby's reaction.

LANGUAGE SKILLS

Have the baby look at her face in the mirror. Talk to the baby about what the two of you see in the mirror.

SOCIAL AND EMOTIONAL

Sing: *"If You are Happy and You Know It."* While you and the baby are looking in the mirror, make the motions to the song and observe the baby's expressions in the mirror.

Theme I: The World Around Me

LARGE MOTOR SKILLS

Look in a mirror. Have two or three hats nearby so that you can put them on the baby's head while she looks at her reflections. Then let the baby put the hats on. Talk to the baby about what she sees.

SMALL MOTOR SKILLS

Sit with the baby before a mirror and touch different parts of your body. Tell the baby what you are touching. Encourage the baby to do the same.

SENSORY PERCEPTION

Make funny faces in the mirror and see if the baby will imitate what you are doing.

LANGUAGE SKILLS

Look in the mirror with the baby and smile. Tell the baby what she is seeing. Show the baby a happy face and a sad face, and reinforce this by saying "Happy, sad." See if the baby imitates you.

SOCIAL AND EMOTIONAL

Have the baby look in the mirror at herself. See if she plays with her own reflection. Encourage the baby to watch other babies in the mirror. Talk about what the baby sees.

FINDING THE NOISE

LARGE MOTOR SKILLS

Stomp your feet on the floor. See if the baby in the crib will turn to look and find the noise.

SMALL MOTOR SKILLS

Crumple up some paper. See if the baby will look to find the noise. See if the baby will help you crumple the paper.

SENSORY PERCEPTION

Stand behind the baby. Clap your hands together and see if the baby turns to find the noise.

LANGUAGE SKILLS

Play the game: "Where is It?" To do this, make a noise with a toy, then hide it. Look at the baby and say, "Where is it?"

SOCIAL AND EMOTIONAL

Make noise with a musical toy. Observe if the baby looks to find the noise. Do this with a small group on the floor. Enthusiastically encourage them to look and find the noise.

LARGE MOTOR SKILLS

Stomp your feet on the floor. See if the baby will find the noise. Encourage the baby to copy you. Say the baby's name. Then ask the child to "stomp" her feet.

SMALL MOTOR SKILLS

Crumple up paper behind your back. Check to see if the baby will go behind you to find the noise. Encourage her to crumple the paper to make the same noise.

SENSORY PERCEPTION

Call to the baby by name before coming into her view. Let the baby try to find the person calling her name.

LANGUAGE SKILLS

Record the baby's sounds. Play the tape back for the baby to hear.

SOCIAL AND EMOTIONAL

Sing: *"Here's the Train"* (Every Day in Every Way). Encourage mobile babies to move around as you sing.

PEEK-A-BOO

LARGE MOTOR SKILLS

Put something over your face. Then take it off and say, "Peek-a-boo." Observe the baby's reaction. Move around when you play this game and observe if the baby looks around or moves to see you.

SMALL MOTOR SKILLS

Show the baby a toy. Hide it behind your back and say, "Peek-a- boo." Show the toy again. When you show the toy, let the baby touch or grab it. Do this several times.

SENSORY PERCEPTION

Cover your face with your hands, then uncover it as you say, "Peek-a-boo." Then, put your hands gently over the baby's face (leave plenty of space), then uncover as you say, "Peek-a-boo." Alternate covering your face and the baby's face.

LANGUAGE SKILLS

Read a Peek-a-Boo Book.

SOCIAL AND EMOTIONAL

Say and act out this rhyme to the baby: *"Peek-A-Boo"* (Finger Frolics). Give the baby hugs.

LARGE MOTOR SKILLS

Hide a sound-making toy behind your back. Let the baby listen to the music. See if she will go around behind you to find the toy. Show her the toy and say, "Peek-A-Boo."

SMALL MOTOR SKILLS

Put a block on the floor, with the baby watching. Place a large box over it to cover it. See if the baby can find the toy. Say, "Where is the block?" Uncover it and say, "Peek-A-Boo." Help the baby to uncover the block herself.

SENSORY PERCEPTION

Show the baby a big, bright, clear, real photo of an animal. Cover the picture with a cloth and say, "Where did it go?" Uncover it and say, "Peek-A-Boo."

LANGUAGE SKILLS

Place a favorite food behind the baby's dish when she is seated in her high chair. See if she will find the food. Say, "I'm looking for the fruit." When it is found, say, "Peek-A-Boo."

SOCIAL AND EMOTIONAL

When family comes to pick the baby up, encourage them to play a short game of "Peek-A-Boo" before leaving for the day.

MOVING OBJECTS

LARGE MOTOR SKILLS

Move the hanging mobile over the baby's bed back and forth. See if the baby looks toward the moving object.

SMALL MOTOR SKILLS

Let the baby play with toy keys.

SENSORY PERCEPTION

Shake a bell gently over the baby's head and see if she will turn to find the object. Watch to see if the baby finds the sound.

LANGUAGE SKILLS

Sing: *"Jingle Bear."* (Early Childhood Curriculum Resource Book)

SOCIAL AND EMOTIONAL"

Sing to the baby: *"Clap your hands."* (Early Childhood Curriculum Resource Book)

LARGE MOTOR SKILLS

Stand in front of a mirror with the baby and move your body in a lot of different ways. See if the baby will copy you.

SMALL MOTOR SKILLS

Tie a long string on several toys. See if the baby will reach for the toys. Talk about what she is doing.

SENSORY PERCEPTION

Sit with the baby on the floor on a bright sunny day. Show the baby how the sunlight shines on the floor. Wave your hand over the light to make shadows move. Tell her what she sees.

LANGUAGE SKILLS

Put some bells in a plastic bottle. Let the baby shake the bottle and talk about the moving objects.

SOCIAL AND EMOTIONAL

Sing to the baby: *"Moving Song."* (Early Childhood Curriculum Resource Book)

All My Senses

THEME II

MOUTHING

LARGE MOTOR SKILLS

Put the baby's teething ring in a sealable plastic bag and place in the refrigerator to get cold. Remove it from the bag and give it to the baby to chew on. Talk about the cold feeling. Be sure to sanitize the teething ring after use.

SMALL MOTOR SKILLS

Place a rattle in the baby's hand. Replace or offer different rattles several times. Observe the baby as she mouths the rattles. Talk to the baby about what is happening. Be sure to sanitize the rattles after use.

SENSORY PERCEPTION

Gently shake a rattle over the baby's head. Give the baby the rattle. Observe and talk to the baby about what she is doing. Talk about the different textures she might feel on her mouth.

LANGUAGE SKILLS

Recite: *"Little Miss Muffet."*

SOCIAL AND EMOTIONAL

Give kisses on hands and cheeks. Offer your hand or cheek so that the baby can try to give you a kiss. Be sure to wash yours and the baby's hands before and after this activity.

LARGE MOTOR SKILLS

While feeding the baby, talk about what she is eating. Encourage the baby to feed herself.

SMALL MOTOR SKILLS

Give the baby her teething ring to chew on. Sanitize after use.

SENSORY PERCEPTION

Give the baby her teething toy to mouth on. Use one with a variety of textures. Tell baby what she is feeling. Sanitize after use.

LANGUAGE SKILLS

Read the story: *"Eat Up Dudley"* by David Wojtowyer.

SOCIAL AND EMOTIONAL

Use personal rattles and teethers from home. For babies that are teething, let them chew on the teethers and let others shake rattles.

WHAT DO YOU HEAR?

INFANTS 0-6 MONTHS

LARGE MOTOR SKILLS

Lay the baby down and shake a rattle around her head. See if the baby will turn to find the sound.

SMALL MOTOR SKILLS

Shake a rattle and let the baby hear the sound. See if the baby will look for or find it and shake it.

SENSORY PERCEPTION

Make different sounds with toys, your mouth, etc. Ask, "What do you hear?" Tell the baby what you hear.

LANGUAGE SKILLS

Talk in different pitches with your voice. See if the baby hears the differences. Observe the baby's reactions.

SOCIAL AND EMOTIONAL

Make happy sounds. Watch to see if the baby notices. Talk about how it feels to be happy and what there is to be happy about.

LARGE MOTOR SKILLS

Call to the baby from a different place in the room. See if the baby hears you. Encourage the baby to come to you.

SMALL MOTOR SKILLS

Make a noise with your mouth. See if the baby repeats it. When the baby makes a noise, repeat it.

SENSORY PERCEPTION

Talk and sing to the baby using different pitches in your voice. Use low, soft, high pitches, but not any that would scare the baby.

LANGUAGE SKILLS

Use instruments. Shake the instruments and sing. Try to get the baby to copy what you do. Give the baby the toy. Say, "Shake your toy."

SOCIAL AND EMOTIONAL

Sing, *"This Is The Way We Shake Our Instruments"* (Early Childhood Curriculum Resource Book). Encourage the babies to join in and shake the instruments.

FEELING

LARGE MOTOR SKILLS

Lay a soft blanket on the mat and put the baby on it. Encourage the baby to lift her head, chest and to roll over. Say, "That feels good and soft."

SMALL MOTOR SKILLS

Lay your finger in the baby's hand. Let the baby hold on to your finger.

SENSORY PERCEPTION

Hold the baby facing you. Smile at the baby and say, " I see your happy face, see my happy face." Let the baby feel your cheeks when you smile and release your smile.

LANGUAGE SKILLS

Walk the baby around the room and outdoors. Help the baby touch things and talk about how they feel–textures, colors, temperatures.

SOCIAL AND EMOTIONAL

Cuddle the baby and give hugs. Let other adults give hugs to the baby.

LARGE MOTOR SKILLS

Make feelie bags by putting some gel into a sealable plastic bag and secure it by taping over the lip part. Encourage the baby to squeeze the bag. Talk about how the bag feels. Take off the baby's shoes and let her step on the bag. Talk about how the bag feels. Observe the baby's reactions.

SMALL MOTOR SKILLS

Put several materials and textures inside a box. Let the baby feel inside the box, and feel the box for different textures. Talk to the baby about how the materials feel – soft, rough, or bumpy.

SENSORY PERCEPTION

Use personal stuffed animals from home for babies to hug and touch.

LANGUAGE SKILLS

Let the baby feel and rub stuffed animals. Talk about how they feel soft to the baby. Encourage the baby to say the words.

SOCIAL AND EMOTIONAL

Make Jell-O pudding. Let the babies see how it feels.

BOOK OF SMELLS

LARGE MOTOR SKILLS

Take the baby outside after a rain. Talk about the new smells.

SMALL MOTOR SKILLS

Spray a mild spice or vanilla extract on your neck. Hold the baby where she can be near the smell. Talk to the baby about the smell.

SENSORY PERCEPTION

Talk to the baby about the smell of baby powder. Breathe deeply through your nose as the baby watches. Talk about the smell.

LANGUAGE SKILLS

Read *"What's That Smell?"* by Janelle Cherington.

SOCIAL AND EMOTIONAL

Have parents bring something from home that has a particular smell. Make up a song about it.

LARGE MOTOR SKILLS

Put vanilla, lemon, or almond extract on cotton balls. Tie them up in some material and let the baby smell them. Talk about the smells.

SMALL MOTOR SKILLS

Talk about the different smells in a book. Let the baby put her hand on the pictures.

SENSORY PERCEPTION

Put two cotton balls in a plastic soda bottle. Sprinkle them with different spices. Give the plastic soda bottle to the baby to smell. Talk about the smells.

LANGUAGE SKILLS

Read, *"What's That Smell?"* by Janelle Cherington.

SOCIAL AND EMOTIONAL

Have parents bring something from home that has a particular smell. Make up a song about it.

JACK IN THE BOX

LARGE MOTOR SKILLS

Sit with the baby and a Jack in the Box in your lap. Wind up the Jack in the Box. When Jack pops out, throw your hands up and say, "Pop."

SMALL MOTOR SKILLS

Turn the knob on the Jack in the Box. Encourage the baby to touch the knob.

SENSORY PERCEPTION

Sing: *"Pop Goes The Weasel."* Use actions with the song.

LANGUAGE SKILLS

Tell the baby about Jack in the Box popping up.

SOCIAL AND EMOTIONAL

Sing: *"Jack in the Box, Pop Goes Jack"* (Early Childhood Curriculum Resource Book).

LARGE MOTOR SKILLS

Sit with the baby and a Jack in the Box on the floor. Turn the knob. When Jack pops out, say, "Jack popped out of the box." Encourage the baby to the turn the knob. Try to get the baby to throw her hands in the air when "Jack" pops out.

SMALL MOTOR SKILLS

Sitting with the baby and Jack in the Box on the floor, place the baby's hand on the knob. Put your hand over the baby's hand. Turn the knob. Talk about what you are doing.

SENSORY PERCEPTION

Sing: *"Pop Goes The Weasel."* Encourage the baby to act out the song. Use the baby's name in the song.

LANGUAGE SKILLS

Talk to the baby about Jack popping out of the box. Encourage the baby to say the word "pop."

SOCIAL AND EMOTIONAL

Sing: *"Jack in the Box, Pop Goes Jack"* (Early Childhood Curriculum Resource Book).

All Kinds of Good Touches

Theme III

STROKING

LARGE MOTOR SKILLS

Place your hand on your face. Move your hand across your nose, mouth, hair, and eyes. Say the name of each body part as you stroke it. Place the baby's hand over your hand so that the baby's arms will move with you.

SMALL MOTOR SKILLS

Stroke the baby's fingers and toes and chant about what you are stroking.

SENSORY PERCEPTION

Gently stroke the baby's leg or arm as you hum softly. Talk with the baby about the feelings.

LANGUAGE SKILLS

Read: *"Mommy Hugs"* by Maryann Cocca-Leffler.

SOCIAL AND EMOTIONAL

Hold the baby in your arms and stroke her legs as you talk to her. Observe if the baby is playing with your fingers and hands.

LARGE MOTOR SKILLS

Have the baby lie on her back in your lap with her head at your knees. Encourage the baby to play with her hands and feet. Say a chant about what the baby is doing.

SMALL MOTOR SKILLS

Put fuzzy fabrics around the baby's bottle and encourage her to stroke it. Observe the baby's reaction.

SENSORY PERCEPTION

Lay the baby on her back. Sing familiar songs while you are stroking her leg. Encourage the baby to do the same.

LANGUAGE SKILLS

Read: *"Daddy Hugs"* by Maryann Cocca-Leffler.

SOCIAL AND EMOTIONAL

Sing to the baby: *"I Love You"* (Every Day in Every Way). Hold the baby close to you while you quietly hum and stroke the baby.

MASSAGING

LARGE MOTOR SKILLS

While changing the baby's diaper, massage the baby's leg as you say loving words to her. Say, "I'm massaging your smooth legs," etc. Help the baby move her legs around.

SMALL MOTOR SKILLS

Hold and massage the baby's hands and arms as you talk to the baby, telling her what you are doing.

SENSORY PERCEPTION

Rub the baby's tummy lightly as you hold the baby and sing lullabies.

LANGUAGE SKILLS

Massage the baby's fingers as you say the rhyme: *One Little, Two Little, Three Little Babies* (Early Childhood Curriculum Resource Book).

SOCIAL AND EMOTIONAL

With the baby on her stomach, massage the baby's back and legs. Tell the baby what you are doing. Put the baby in her bed close to you while you do your daily chores. As you wipe the table and put things away, sing to the baby about what you are doing. Repeat the same phrase several times.

LARGE MOTOR SKILLS

Have the baby lay on her back on a mat on the floor, and massage the baby's feet. Tell the baby what you are doing. Encourage the baby to rub her feet.

SMALL MOTOR SKILLS

Give the baby a doll or stuffed animal and show her how to massage the toy's back. Encourage the baby to massage the toy.

SENSORY PERCEPTION

Pick up the baby, supporting her firmly around her middle. Swing her gently through the air. Talk to her about what is happening.

LANGUAGE SKILLS

Sing: *"One Little, Two Little, Three Little Babies"* (Early Childhood Curriculum Resource Book).

SOCIAL AND EMOTIONAL

Stroke and massage the baby as you hum a quiet song.

HOLDING

LARGE MOTOR SKILLS

Hold the baby in your lap facing away from you, and hold the baby's hands. Clap, wiggle her fingers and make shapes in the air.

SMALL MOTOR SKILLS

Gently pull a long scarf or string across the palm of the baby's hand. Encourage the baby to close her hands around the scarf and hold on to it.

SENSORY PERCEPTION

Pick up the baby. Walk around; tell the baby what is in the environment.

LANGUAGE SKILLS

Hold the baby up to look out the window. Talk to the baby about what she sees.

SOCIAL AND EMOTIONAL

Lay your finger in the baby's hand. See if she will hold on to your finger.

LARGE MOTOR SKILLS

Hold the baby on your lap, and rock her from side to side. Hug the baby. Let the baby hug you back.

SMALL MOTOR SKILLS

Hold the baby on your lap while you do *"Pat-A-Cake."* Encourage the baby to clap her hands together.

SENSORY PERCEPTION

Sit with the baby in your lap facing you. Firmly hold her under her arms and move the baby back and forth from a lying down to a sitting up position while you chant or sing a song. Be sure to make lots of eye contact with the baby

LANGUAGE SKILLS

Hold the baby and read a story. Encourage the baby to hold a favorite toy and read a story.

SOCIAL AND EMOTIONAL

Encourage the baby to hold and rock a doll.

ROCKING

LARGE MOTOR SKILLS

Rock the baby in the rocker at different speeds (not too fast). Talk about what is happening.

SMALL MOTOR SKILLS

Give the baby a small, soft toy to grasp while rocking back and forth.

SENSORY PERCEPTION

Rock the baby back and forth as you hum, *"Rock-a-Bye Baby."*

LANGUAGE SKILLS

Read a story that involves rocking or make a book about rocking to read.

SOCIAL AND EMOTIONAL

Hold the baby in your arms, and rock her while singing the lullaby: *"Rock-a-Bye Baby"* (Every Day in Every Way).

LARGE MOTOR SKILLS

Give the baby a doll to rock. Encourage the baby to rock it herself in the baby rocking chair.

SMALL MOTOR SKILLS

Give the baby a toy she can hold. Encourage her to hold the toy and rock back and forth.

SENSORY PERCEPTION

Place different textures of cloth over the baby's rocking chair for the baby to feel.

LANGUAGE SKILLS

Talk to the baby about what she is doing as she rocks in the rocking chair. Say, "Rocking." See if the baby will repeat the word.

SOCIAL AND EMOTIONAL

Sing: *"Rock-a-Bye Baby"* as you rock the baby in your arms on a mat or in the rocking chair. Talk softly and gently to the baby.

BOUNCING

LARGE MOTOR SKILLS

Stand the baby up on your legs with your hands under her arms. Gently raise the baby up and slowly let her down.

SMALL MOTOR SKILLS

Lay the baby on her tummy on a mat. Place a medium round rubber ball in front of her. Bat the ball to make it bounce. Encourage the baby to do the same.

SENSORY PERCEPTION

Bounce a stuffed animal up and down on your arm or leg. Talk about how it feels.

LANGUAGE SKILLS

Read: "Baby Things" by Catherine and Laurence Anholt.

SOCIAL AND EMOTIONAL

Sing: "Bouncing Song" (Early Childhood Curriculum Resource Book). With the baby on your knees, gently raise your knees up and slowly let your knees down.

LARGE MOTOR SKILLS

Sit the baby on your lap facing you. Chant and gently raise the baby up and slowly lower her down. Smile and laugh a lot with the baby. Say, "Bouncy, bouncy."

SMALL MOTOR SKILLS

Bounce a ball. Encourage the baby to bounce the ball. Talk to the baby about what the ball is doing.

SENSORY PERCEPTION

Lay the baby on a thick mat. Push up and down gently on the thick mat to make the baby bounce.

LANGUAGE SKILLS

Read a book about bouncing.

SOCIAL AND EMOTIONAL

Sing: *"Bouncing Song"* (Early Childhood Curriculum Resource Book). With the baby on your knees, gently raise your knees up and slowly let your knees down.

46

My Hands and Eyes Can Do Things Together

THEME IV

REACHING

LARGE MOTOR SKILLS

Tie long colorful ribbons around your knees, and shake them. Encourage the baby to reach up to play with the ribbons. Talk about what the baby is doing.

SMALL MOTOR SKILLS

Lay the baby on a mat. Put bright colored objects in front of the baby. Encourage the baby to reach for the objects. Talk about what the baby is doing.

SENSORY PERCEPTION

Place the cradle gym over the baby, and help the baby to reach and hit at it with her hand.

LANGUAGE SKILLS

Put a toy in front of the baby, then reach and say, "Reach, reach." Ask her, "Can you reach it? I see you reaching for it. You reached it."

SOCIAL AND EMOTIONAL

Reach to pick up the baby. Observe to see if the baby reaches out her arms to be picked up.

LARGE MOTOR SKILLS

Put a ball in front of the baby. Encourage the baby to reach for the ball and roll it to you.

SMALL MOTOR SKILLS

Blow bubbles in the air above the baby's head, and see if the baby will reach for the bubbles. Encourage her to do so.

SENSORY PERCEPTION

Hang up a beach ball. Swing the ball back and forth. See if the baby will reach out and swipe at the ball.

LANGUAGE SKILLS

Read the baby's personal baby book made by her family. Encourage the baby to repeat words. For example: "Mommy," "Daddy," "Yes," "No," "Eat More." Do sign language, too.

SOCIAL AND EMOTIONAL

Game: Stretch, Stretch. Stretch up, stretch down. Encourage the baby to stretch up and down. Be enthusiastic about her efforts. Observe and encourage parallel play.

GRASPING

LARGE MOTOR SKILLS

Hold a toy above the baby's head. Encourage the baby to grab the toy. Let the baby play with the toy when she grabs it. Talk to the baby about the toy.

SMALL MOTOR SKILLS

Place a small soft toy or block in the baby's hand for the baby to hold on to. Talk to the baby about the toy.

SENSORY PERCEPTION

Place your finger in the baby's hand. See if she grasps your finger.

LANGUAGE SKILLS

Have cloth books and soft books for the baby to grasp. Talk to the baby about her grasping the books.

SOCIAL AND EMOTIONAL

Rhyme: *"I'll Grasp Yours"* (Early Childhood Curriculum Resource Book).

LARGE MOTOR SKILLS

Sit with the baby and give her a snap bead toy. When she has a good grasp, give her a second toy. Help the baby join the beads together. Say, "Take the other bead now and join the beads together."

SMALL MOTOR SKILLS

Give the baby a small toy. See if the baby will change the toy from one hand to the other. Be enthusiastic about her efforts. Also encourage the baby to grasp the spoon when eating.

SENSORY PERCEPTION

Give the baby blocks of different shapes, colors, and textures to grasp. Talk to the baby about the blocks. Put dry cereal on a high chair tray to let the baby perfect her thumb and forefinger grasp.

LANGUAGE SKILLS

Read a book about things that go.

SOCIAL AND EMOTIONAL

With the help of another caregiver, seat yourself behind a baby that is sitting on the floor. Using a small blanket or towel, you and baby can play "Tug-O-War" with the other caregiver.

TAKING APART

INFANTS 0-6 MONTHS

LARGE MOTOR SKILLS

Take giant interlocking blocks and pull them apart while the baby is looking. Say "pop" when you pull them apart.

SMALL MOTOR SKILLS

Take colored interlocking cubes, and put the baby on your lap. Pull the cubes apart and say "pop."

SENSORY PERCEPTION

Give the baby interlocking cubes, and help her pull on them. Say, "Pull the cubes apart."

LANGUAGE SKILLS

Read books about taking things apart.

SOCIAL AND EMOTIONAL

Sing: *"Taking Apart."* (Early Childhood Curriculum Resource Book)

LARGE MOTOR SKILLS

Give the baby two cubes to pull apart. See if the baby is able to pull them apart on her first try. If so, add more. Be enthusiastic about her efforts.

SMALL MOTOR SKILLS

Sit the baby on your lap. Place two pop beads joined together in the baby's hands. Place your hands over the baby's hands and pull the beads apart. Say "pop " as you pull.

SENSORY PERCEPTION

Give the baby two pop beads that are connected, one in each hand. Put your hands over her hands and help her pull the beads apart. Encourage the baby to repeat the action.

LANGUAGE SKILLS

Read books about taking apart.

SOCIAL AND EMOTIONAL

Sing to the baby, *"Take Your Little Hands"* (Early Childhood Curriculum Resource Book). Show and talk about how everyone's hands fit together and come apart.

FITTING TOGETHER

LARGE MOTOR SKILLS

Take giant interlocking blocks and fit them together while the baby is looking. Say, "Can you make it fit?"

SMALL MOTOR SKILLS

Take cubes and push them together as the baby is looking. Say, "I'm pushing the cubes together."

SENSORY PERCEPTION

Do a ring stack. Give the rings to the baby and help her stack them.

LANGUAGE SKILLS

Encourage the baby to make the rings fit. Say, "Would you like to try to make it fit?" Give the baby big blocks or beads and observe her.

SOCIAL AND EMOTIONAL

Sing: *"I Can Fit It Together,"* (Early Childhood Curriculum Resource Book).

Theme IV: My Hands and Eyes Can Do Things Together

LARGE MOTOR SKILLS

Put two large items together by pulling or pushing. Let the baby help you.

SMALL MOTOR SKILLS

Join large items together by pushing them together. Say, "Good" and encourage the baby to do it all by herself. Fit together a three-piece puzzle.

SENSORY PERCEPTION

Sit the baby on a mat. Use coffee cans with shapes cut in the lid and sort objects by shapes.

LANGUAGE SKILLS

Place large pegs on a peg board. Talk about what you are doing. Encourage and assist the baby to do the same. Tell the baby what she is doing.

SOCIAL AND EMOTIONAL

Help the baby snap together large beads to make a necklace. Put the necklace on and off the baby. Do the same with other babies. You can also join together building cubes and giant blocks.

Make My Brain Work

T HEME V

HIDE AND SEEK

INFANTS 0-6 MONTHS

LARGE MOTOR SKILLS

With the baby and her favorite stuffed animal in your arms, cover the stuffed animal and then put it in the baby's arms. Say, "Here it is."

SMALL MOTOR

With the baby on your lap, squeak a squeaky toy. Cover it with a blanket, then uncover it and squeak it again. Say, "There it is." Let the baby touch the toy.

SENSORY PERCEPTION

Rock the baby back and forth. As you rock forward, look down at the baby and say, "I see you."

LANGUAGE SKILLS

Show the baby a bright clear photo of a real animal. Cover the picture with a cloth. Uncover it and say, "Hide and Seek."

SOCIAL AND EMOTIONAL

Play hide and seek with the babies. Hold one baby in your arms and face another baby, then say to the baby you are facing, "We see you." Then turn away and turn back and say, "We're back."

Theme V: Make My Brain Work

LARGE MOTOR SKILLS

Roll a ball out of the baby's reach and view and encourage her to creep and find it.

SMALL MOTOR SKILLS

Hide a toy beneath a cloth or a box. See if the baby finds it.

SENSORY PERCEPTION

While the baby is watching, hide a cracker under a cup. Let the baby find the cracker and eat it. Praise the child when she finds the cracker.

LANGUAGE SKILLS

Play the hide and seek game. (Early Childhood Curriculum Resource Book).

SOCIAL AND EMOTIONAL

Hide behind a chair. Look out and say, "I see you." Encourage the baby to hide behind the chair. Play with more than one baby at a time.

WAVE-BYE-BYE

LARGE MOTOR SKILLS

When the teacher waves to the baby, encourage the baby to wave back by moving the baby's hand. Repeat this action.

SMALL MOTOR SKILLS

Wave bye-bye to the baby. Encourage the baby to wave back. This will increase small motor control.

SENSORY PERCEPTION

As parents pick up their children from the center, wave bye-bye and see if the baby will wave back.

LANGUAGE SKILLS

Sing: *"Bye-Bye"* (Early Childhood Curriculum Resource Book). Wave to the baby as you sing the song.

SOCIAL AND EMOTIONAL

Play the waving game. Say the baby's name and wave to her and see if the baby does the same back.

LARGE MOTOR SKILLS

Stand at different places in the room and let the baby wave to you.

SMALL MOTOR SKILLS

Encourage the baby to wave bye-bye to parents, teachers, and friends.

SENSORY PERCEPTION

Encourage the baby to wave bye-bye.

LANGUAGE SKILLS

Encourage babies to wave and say, "Bye-bye."

SOCIAL AND EMOTIONAL

Encourage parents and other visitors to the room to wave bye-bye to the baby and and say "I'll be back."

SCRIBBLING

LARGE MOTOR SKILLS

Place pudding in a pan or on wax paper. Put the baby's feet in the pudding, and help her "walk" through it. Then place the baby's feet on a clean sheet of paper to make prints. You can write her name on the paper and then keep or display it.

SMALL MOTOR SKILLS

Place some pudding in a pan. Put the baby's hands in the pudding. Encourage the baby to do the same. Let her "draw" with the pudding on a clean sheet of paper. Place the baby's hands on a clean sheet of paper to make prints. Write her name on it and then keep or display.

SENSORY PERCEPTION

Get a large, fat crayon. Help the baby hold the crayon and guide her hand to scribble on some paper.

LANGUAGE SKILLS

While the baby is watching, write her name on a sheet of paper while saying "Look, I'm writing your name."

SOCIAL AND EMOTIONAL

Sing: *"This is the Way We Scribble"* (Early Childhood Curriculum Resource Book).

LARGE MOTOR SKILLS

Take a big sheet of paper and tape it to the floor. Put the baby on the floor next to it. Draw lines with large crayons on the paper as the baby looks on, and encourage the baby to do the same.

SMALL MOTOR SKILLS

Take a big sheet of paper and put it on the baby's tray. Draw lines with large crayons on the paper as the baby looks on. Then encourage the baby to do the same.

SENSORY PERCEPTION

Create a drawing by scribbling on a shirt with some puff paint. After it dries, let the baby feel your creation and follow the lines with her fingers.

LANGUAGE SKILLS

Take a sheet of paper and a large crayon and let the baby scribble. Then say, "We are writing your name."

SOCIAL AND EMOTIONAL

Sing: *"This is the Way We Write Our Name"* (Early Childhood Curriculum Resource Book).

PAT-A-CAKE

LARGE MOTOR SKILLS

Clap your hands together and say, "Clap-clap-clap." Gently clap the baby's hands together.

SMALL MOTOR SKILLS

Sing finger play songs using any finger play book. Move your fingers as the songs tell you, then hold the baby's hands or feet and move her body as you sing.

SENSORY PERCEPTION

Make a "cake" with Play-Doh® and let the baby touch and pat it while you hold it in your hand.

LANGUAGE SKILLS

Read: *"Pat-a-Cake"* (Early Childhood Curriculum Resource Book). Do the actions.

SOCIAL AND EMOTIONAL

Say, *"Pat-a-Cake."* Observe the baby and encourage her to do the actions.

LARGE MOTOR SKILLS

Clap your hands together and say, "Pat-a-Cake." Encourage the baby to clap her hands together.

SMALL MOTOR SKILLS

Clap your hands and see if the baby will copy you.

SENSORY PERCEPTION

Say the rhyme, "Pat-a-Cake" and move to the words. Repeat and see if the baby joins in. Use a "cake" made out of Play-Doh® to add to the movements.

LANGUAGE SKILLS

Encourage the baby to say the words, "Pat-a-Cake," as she sings.

SOCIAL AND EMOTIONAL

Sing the Song: "Pat-a-Cake." Observe and encourage the baby to do the actions.

See What My Hands Can Do

T<small>HEME</small> VI

SQUEEZING

LARGE MOTOR SKILLS

Give the baby a large, soft squeeze toy to squeeze.

SMALL MOTOR SKILLS

Give the baby a variety of small, soft squeeze toys to play with.

SENSORY PERCEPTION

Make a "snake" out of Play-Doh® and let the baby squeeze it in her palm.

LANGUAGE SKILLS

Say: *"Ten Little Fingers."* (Early Childhood Curriculum Resource Book).

SOCIAL AND EMOTIONAL

Say and do the finger play, *"Open, Shut Them"* (Early Childhood Curriculum Resource Book).

LARGE MOTOR SKILLS

Make some squeeze bags by putting gel, jello, rice, etc. in sealable plastic bags and securing the open end. Squeeze the bags. Give the bags to the baby, and encourage her to play with the bags.

SMALL MOTOR SKILLS

Help the baby play in a small pool or tub with half an inch of water. Give her small cups to fill and pour, spoons to stir the water, and sponges to squeeze. Talk with her about what she's doing. For variety, use colored water and sponges in multicultural colors or people shapes.

SENSORY PERCEPTION

Give the baby a variety of rubber squeeze toys to play with.

LANGUAGE SKILLS

Go around the room and find things to squeeze. Every time you squeeze something say the word "squeeze." Use different tones of voice.

SOCIAL AND EMOTIONAL

Say and do the finger play, *"Open, Shut Them."* (Early Childhood Curriculum Resource Book). See if the baby will do the actions.

RELEASING

INFANTS 0-6 MONTHS

LARGE MOTOR SKILLS

Show a toy to the baby. Encourage the baby to reach and grasp the toy.
Help older babies release the toy into a container.

SMALL MOTOR SKILLS

Place soft blocks where the baby can reach them. See if the baby will
pick up and release them.

SENSORY PERCEPTION

When the baby picks up a toy and has it in her hand, give the baby
another toy. Encourage the baby to release the first toy to take the toy
you are giving her.

LANGUAGE SKILLS

Say, " *Ten Little Fingers*" (Early Childhood Curriculum Resource Book).

SOCIAL AND EMOTIONAL

Sing to the baby: *"This is the Way We Clean Up"* (Early Childhood
Curriculum Resource Book).

LARGE MOTOR SKILLS

Put one block or toy in the baby's hand. Give the baby another toy. See if she will release one to get the other one.

SMALL MOTOR SKILLS

Place crackers on the baby's high chair tray. Encourage the baby to use pincher movement to pick up the crumbs and release them into her mouth.

SENSORY PERCEPTION

Cut a hole in the top of a box. Then give the baby a safe small toy to release into the box. Shake the box around and listen to the sound of the object moving inside.

LANGUAGE SKILLS

Read picture books with real photos. Look at the pictures. Point to the pictures, and say the picture word. Encourage the baby to say the word. When turning the pages, encourage the baby to help turn and release the pages.

SOCIAL AND EMOTIONAL

Sing to the baby: *"This is the Way We Clean Up"* (Early Childhood Curriculum Resource Book).

DROPPING

LARGE MOTOR SKILLS

Drop a rattle by the baby's side. See if the baby looks to see where it was dropped.

SMALL MOTOR SKILLS

While the baby is sitting in her seat, drop a few drops of water on the palm of her hand. See if she moves her hand or looks at the water.

SENSORY PERCEPTION

Give the baby different sizes of shapes to hold. Talk about the shapes. Let the baby watch while you drop them into a bucket. Listen to the sounds and talk about what you hear.

LANGUAGE SKILLS

Say: *"Ten Little Fingers."* (Early Childhood Curriculum Resource Book)

SOCIAL AND EMOTIONAL

Let the baby watch you drop small items and say, "Uh-oh." Then pick up an item and say, "It's okay," and hand it to the baby.

LARGE MOTOR SKILLS

While the baby stands holding onto your legs, drop a noise-making toy onto the floor. See if the baby turns to see what was dropped.

SMALL MOTOR SKILLS

Cut a hole in the top of a box. Then give the baby some small, safe toys to drop in the box.

SENSORY PERCEPTION

Drop the same item on many different surfaces (i.e. carpet, tile, wood, a table, grass, dirt, etc.) and listen to the sounds. Talk about the sounds.

LANGUAGE SKILLS

Say: *"Ten Little Fingers."* (Early Childhood Curriculum Resource Book)

SOCIAL AND EMOTIONAL

Give the baby clothespins to drop into a plastic jug. Do this with other babies in a group. Enthusiastically encourage their efforts.

AIMING

LARGE MOTOR SKILLS

Sit with the baby on a soft area. Show her a toy and lay the toy down. Encourage the baby to turn and find the toy.

SMALL MOTOR SKILLS

Place the baby on her stomach. Place a toy in front of her. Encourage her to reach for the toy.

SENSORY PERCEPTION

Give a toy to the baby. Hold your hand out. See if she can drop the toy in your hand.

LANGUAGE SKILLS

Make and read, *"Black and White Books"* by putting black pictures on white paper and white pictures on black paper. Point to interesting pictures in the book.

SOCIAL AND EMOTIONAL

Sing to the baby: *"This is the Way We Aim."*
(Early Childhood Curriculum Resource Book)

LARGE MOTOR SKILLS

Sit on the floor with the baby and toss a toy out in front of her. Encourage the baby to go after the toy and bring it back. Make a bean bag toss, and encourage the baby to throw the bean bags through a large hole in a box.

SMALL MOTOR SKILLS

Drop small cubes in a container. Help the baby reach in and grab the toys and pull them out.

SENSORY PERCEPTION

Find toys that are the same shape, but different sizes and textures, for the baby to hold and feel, and have her drop them into a container.

LANGUAGE SKILLS

Say: *"Ten Little Fingers."* (Early Childhood Curriculum Resource Book)

SOCIAL AND EMOTIONAL

Hold clothespins over the opening of a plastic bottle and drop the clothespin into the bottle. Encourage the baby to do the same. Enthusiastically encourage her efforts. Make it a group game.

Let's
Communicate

T<small>HEME</small> VII

GURGLING AND BABBLE TALK

INFANTS 0-6 MONTHS

LARGE MOTOR SKILLS

Hold the baby and when she makes a noise, move her arm or leg.
Help her dance to her own music.

SMALL MOTOR SKILLS

Click your tongue. Encourage the baby to imitate you.

SENSORY PERCEPTION

Stick out your tongue. Make throaty sounds. Observe the baby's expressions.

LANGUAGE SKILLS

"Coo" and "ca" with the baby. Make the noises the baby makes.
See if the baby will make the noises you make.

SOCIAL AND EMOTIONAL

Put a play telephone up to the baby's ear and pretend to talk to the
baby.

LARGE MOTOR SKILLS

Make a tape of the babies babbling and gurgling. Play back the tape. Give the babies room to "dance to the music" – show them how.

SMALL MOTOR SKILLS

Make throaty sounds. See if the baby will imitate you. Put the baby's hand on your neck so she can feel how you make the sounds.

SENSORY PERCEPTION

Stick out your tongue. Make a noise. Encourage the baby to imitate you.

LANGUAGE SKILLS

"Coo" and "ca" with the baby. Make the noises the baby makes. See if the baby will make the noises you make.

SOCIAL AND EMOTIONAL

Sing: *"This Little Pig."* (Early Childhood Curriculum Resource Book)

FUNNY FACE

LARGE MOTOR SKILLS

Make a mobile of similar faces by drawing on different colored paper. Hang this above the bed, changing table or on the ceiling. Talk to the baby about the mobile.

SMALL MOTOR SKILLS

Cut out big pictures of faces. Put them in any open space at the baby's level. Talk to the baby about the pictures. Encourage the baby to point at or touch the pictures.

SENSORY PERCEPTION

Talk to the baby while feeding and diapering. Make funny faces. Observe the baby's reactions.

LANGUAGE SKILLS

Read: *"Funny Faces"* by Todd Parr.

SOCIAL AND EMOTIONAL

Sing: *"I Love You"* (Early Childhood Curriculum Resource Book). Look at the baby and make different faces while you sing.

LARGE MOTOR SKILLS

Sit on the floor with the baby and make funny faces. See if the baby will copy you.

SMALL MOTOR SKILLS

Sew brightly colored material to make a face on a sock. Encourage the baby to watch it move and touch it.

SENSORY PERCEPTION

Make a book with different pictures of faces: young, old, boys, girls, with different skin colors. Talk about the features when you look at the book with the baby. Make a different voice to go with each face.

LANGUAGE SKILLS

Read: *"Funny Faces,"* by Todd Par. Act out the story. See if the baby will imitate you.

SOCIAL AND EMOTIONAL

Sing to the baby: *"If You're Happy and You Know It"* (Early Childhood Curriculum Resource Book). Be sure to make happy faces and smile at the baby.

HAPPY SOUNDS

LARGE MOTOR SKILLS

Place a mobile with bells and music making noises over the baby's crib. See if the baby will turn to find the noise.

SMALL MOTOR SKILLS

Gently shake a rattle over the baby's head. See if the baby will turn her head to find the sound. Place a rattle in the baby's hand, and help her shake the rattle.

SENSORY PERCEPTION

Talk to the baby using different soft pitches in your voice. Try singing your words.

LANGUAGE SKILLS

Read: *"Ting-a-Lings!"* by Siobhan Dobbs.

SOCIAL AND EMOTIONAL

While holding the baby, make soft, happy sounds and sing *"Looby Loo"* (Early Childhood Curriculum Resource Book). Watch the baby's expressions.

LARGE MOTOR SKILLS

While the baby stands or is holding onto something, drop a noise making toy onto the floor beside the baby. Encourage her to bend and pick it up.

SMALL MOTOR SKILLS

Give the baby different things to drop into a container, so she can hear different sounds.

SENSORY PERCEPTION

Gently lay the baby down on her back and talk about the sounds she can hear.

LANGUAGE SKILLS

Rhyme: *"If I Were a Train."* (Early Childhood Curriculum Resource Book)

SOCIAL AND EMOTIONAL

Sing: *"If You're Happy and You Know It"* (Early Childhood Curriculum Resource Book).

DO WHAT I SAY

LARGE MOTOR SKILLS

Fold a small blanket in half and roll it tightly into a log shaped cushion. Lay the baby on her stomach over the cushion and say to the baby "Roll back and forth." Help the baby to roll back and forth.

SMALL MOTOR SKILLS

Lay the baby on her stomach on a mat. Place a pop-up toy within the baby's reach. Press a key on the pop-up toy. Say to the baby, "Press the key." Help her press the key.

SENSORY PERCEPTION

Lay the baby on her back on a mat. Lay on the floor so the baby can see you. Shake a rattle and say to the baby, "Listen to the sound." Turn your head as if you are listening.

LANGUAGE SKILLS

Say to the baby "ba, ba, ba" or "ma, ma, ma." Encourage the baby to say "ba, ba, ba" or "ma, ma, ma."

SOCIAL AND EMOTIONAL

Read soft cloth books.

LARGE MOTOR SKILLS

Place pieces of banana on the baby's tray. Take a piece and put it into your mouth. Encourage the baby to do the same by saying, "Eat some banana" and making a motion like you are putting something in your mouth.

SMALL MOTOR SKILLS

Cut up a banana into different sized pieces. Encourage the baby by saying, "Pick up this piece."

SENSORY PERCEPTION

Sit the baby on the floor. Put two blocks on the floor in front of the baby. Place one block on top of the other block and say to the baby, "I am putting this block on top of the other block." Take the block down and say to the baby, "Now you place the block on top of the other block." Encourage and help the baby do it.

LANGUAGE SKILLS

Place pieces of orange on the baby's tray. Take a piece and put it into your mouth. Say, " I'm picking up the orange and putting it in my mouth." Say, "Yum, yum." Help the baby pick up a piece and do what you say.

SOCIAL AND EMOTIONAL

Sing: *"Put Your Finger in the Air"* by Woody Guthrie. Encourage the baby to do what the song says.

Wiggle and Tickle

THEME VIII

HOLD AND TALK TO THE BABY

LARGE MOTOR SKILLS

Place the baby on your shoulder. Then walk around the room talking to the baby about what the other babies are doing.

SMALL MOTOR SKILLS

Hold the baby on your lap. Place a rattle in her hand, and then shake the rattle and say, "This is a rattle."

SENSORY PERCEPTION

Hold the baby on your lap as you and the baby look at pictures in a book. Point to the pictures and say the name of each picture.

LANGUAGE SKILLS

Hold the baby on your lap and talk to the baby about what you are doing in the environment.

SOCIAL AND EMOTIONAL

Sing, "Cootchie, Cootchie, Coo," as you lightly touch the baby under the chin or on the stomach. (Early Childhood Curriculum Resource Book)

LARGE MOTOR SKILLS

Place the baby on a mat. Put a rattle on the other side of the mat. Shake the rattle and lay it down. Encourage the baby to crawl to the rattle by laying next to the baby with your hand on the baby's back.

SMALL MOTOR SKILLS

Lay a rattle down. Ask the baby to give the rattle to you. When she does, pick up the baby and giver her a big hug of encouragement.

SENSORY PERCEPTION

With the baby sitting on a mat, give a doll to her. Say, "Hold the baby." Then tell the baby what she is doing. Help the baby say the words or say them for her, if needed.

LANGUAGE SKILLS

Hold a one-sided conversation with the baby while holding her. Ask questions, show excitement and give answers.

SOCIAL AND EMOTIONAL

Read: *"Love You Forever"* by Robert Munsch.

TICKLE TIME

LARGE MOTOR SKILLS

Hold the baby in your lap. Walk your fingers up the baby's arm, and then tickle her under the chin and say, "tickle, tickle".

SMALL MOTOR SKILLS

With the baby on your lap, move your fingers in the air, making a buzzing sound as you move your fingers. Land your fingers on the baby's tummy with a light tickle.

SENSORY PERCEPTION

While changing the baby's diaper, walk your fingers up baby's legs and tummy and tickle her under the chin. Say, "tickle, tickle."

LANGUAGE SKILLS

Place the baby on a mat and say, "I am going to get you." Then touch the child's tummy lightly with your hand and say, "Tickle, tickle."

SOCIAL AND EMOTIONAL

Sing: *"Tickle Me"* (Early Childhood Curriculum Resource Book). Hold the baby in your lap and do what the tickle song says.

LARGE MOTOR SKILLS

Sit the baby on the mat. Walk your fingers up the baby's back to her shoulders and tickle her under the neck. Say, "Tickle, tickle."

SMALL MOTOR SKILLS

Walk your finger to the baby's palm and say, "Tickle, tickle."

SENSORY PERCEPTION

Hold the baby in your lap. Move your fingers around in the air as you make a buzzing sound. Then tickle the baby on the stomach.

LANGUAGE SKILLS

With the baby on a mat, walk your fingers up the baby's sides and tickle her under the arms. Say, "Tickle, tickle." Encourage the baby to say, "Tickle."

SOCIAL AND EMOTIONAL

Sing: *"Tickle Me"* (Early Childhood Curriculum Resource Book).

WIGGLE WIGGLE

LARGE MOTOR SKILLS

Lay on the floor on a mat on your stomach with the baby lying in front of you. Wiggle your fingers across the floor as you say, "Wiggle wiggle." See if the baby will lift her head to see you.

SMALL MOTOR SKILLS

While changing the baby's diaper, wiggle the baby's toes and fingers while saying, *"Five Little Pigs"* (Early Childhood Curriculum Resource Book).

SENSORY PERCEPTION

With the baby on your lap, wiggle your fingers across the chair, moving closer and closer to the baby. Say, "Here comes the wiggle bug."

LANGUAGE SKILLS

Talk to the baby about the feeling and movement as you are wiggling the baby's toes.

SOCIAL AND EMOTIONAL

Sing:" *Wiggle Wiggle.*" (Early Childhood Curriculum Resource Book) Hold the baby in your lap and do what the wiggle song says.

LARGE MOTOR SKILLS

Move your head back and forth as you say, "Wiggle, wiggle."
Try to get the baby to copy you. Then wiggle her fingers, toes,
ears, and nose.

SMALL MOTOR SKILLS

Put your finger on your nose. Wiggle your finger on your nose and
say, "Wiggle, wiggle." Encourage the baby to do the same. Praise the
baby when she does it.

SENSORY PERCEPTION

Standing up, wiggle different parts of your body as you name them.
Have the baby wiggle also.

LANGUAGE SKILLS

Wiggle the baby's toe. Say, "Toe." See if the baby says "Toe."

SOCIAL AND EMOTIONAL

Sing and do with the baby: *"Wiggle Wiggle"* (Early Childhood
Curriculum Resource Book).

BANGING AND SHAKING

LARGE MOTOR SKILLS

Lay the baby on her back. Shake a rattle gently on one side of her head. Encourage her to turn toward the sound. Give the rattle to her to bang.

SMALL MOTOR SKILLS

Shake a rattle in front of the baby. When you have her attention, move the rattle to one side and then slowly to the other side. See if the baby turns toward the rattle. Place the rattle in the baby's hand. See if the baby shakes the rattle.

SENSORY PERCEPTION

While the baby is sitting in an infant chair, give her some toy keys. When she shakes them, hold another object close to the keys. Listen to the noise and talk about what you hear.

LANGUAGE SKILLS

Encourage the baby to shake a rattle or bang a block. Talk to the baby about what she is doing.

SOCIAL AND EMOTIONAL

Sing: "Shake, Rattle, and Roll" (Early Childhood Curriculum Resource Book). Dance slowly with the baby in your arms to the beat of the music.

LARGE MOTOR SKILLS

Give the baby lids, pans and pots with wooden spoons to bang. Be enthusiastic about her efforts.

SMALL MOTOR SKILLS

Choose a toy, name it and say the sound it makes. Encourage baby to imitate you. Let the baby play with the toy.

SENSORY PERCEPTION

Shake a bell or rattle for the baby to see and hear. See if she will squeal, or shake the rattle again.

LANGUAGE SKILLS

Read: *"Best Friends"* by Alison Davis.

SOCIAL AND EMOTIONAL

Give the babies bangers, spoons, pots and shakers at the same time to form a "band." Play along with the "band."

Splash, Splash

THEME IX

WATER PLAY

LARGE MOTOR SKILLS

Put a few drops of water on the baby's arms and legs. Pat the water off. Encourage the baby to pat the water off herself.

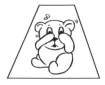

SMALL MOTOR SKILLS

Cup your hand with water in the palm of your hand. Put your hand in front of the baby. Pat the water. Encourage the baby to pat the water.

SENSORY PERCEPTION

Put a few drops of water into the palm of the baby's hand. Then make a splash and tell the baby what you did. Ask and encourage older babies to make a splash.

LANGUAGE SKILLS

Read books about water fun.

SOCIAL AND EMOTIONAL

Sing to the baby: *"Jack and Jill"* (Early Childhood Curriculum Resource Book).

LARGE MOTOR SKILLS

Put an inch of water into a container. Let the baby sit and splash the water. Add toys that float and sink in the water.

SMALL MOTOR SKILLS

Fill a container with water. Help the baby play in the water with her hands and feet.

SENSORY PERCEPTION

Let the baby splash her hand in the water as you say, "Splash, splash." Use a big spoon to splash in the water.

LANGUAGE SKILLS

Let the baby splash in a pie pan of water. Talk about what is happening as she splashes.

SOCIAL AND EMOTIONAL

Sing to the baby: *"Jack and Jill."* (Early Childhood Curriculum Resource Book).

UP OR UNDER

LARGE MOTOR SKILLS

Move the baby from a lying down to a sitting position while you sing.

SMALL MOTOR SKILLS

Talk to the baby about lifting her arms and legs up while her diaper is being changed.

SENSORY PERCEPTION

Hold the baby in your arms and say, "Up, up, goes the baby."
Then put the baby down and say, "Down, down goes the baby."

LANGUAGE SKILLS

Read: *"Baby Things Up and Under"* by Sue Ellis.

SOCIAL AND EMOTIONAL

Say: *" Pat-A-Cake"* (Early Childhood Curriculum Resource Book).

LARGE MOTOR SKILLS

Raise the baby's arms up over her head and say, "Up." Make an obstacle of large soft blocks for the baby to climb up or go down.

SMALL MOTOR SKILLS

Hide a toy under a cloth. Encourage the baby to grab the cloth, and pull it away to find the hidden toy.

SENSORY PERCEPTION

Blow bubbles into the air. Encourage the baby to catch the bubbles.

LANGUAGE SKILLS

Take a small pan, filled with one inch of water, and put the baby's hands under the water as you say, "Under the water." Then pull them out and say, "Up out of the water."

SOCIAL AND EMOTIONAL

Sing; *"The Up and Under"* song (Early Childhood Curriculum Resource Book).

RUB-A-DUB DUB

LARGE MOTOR SKILLS

Put an inch of water in a pan. Remove the baby's shoes and socks. Hold the baby firmly under her arms over the pan of water. Let the baby's feet splash in the water.

SMALL MOTOR SKILLS

Recite the poem, *"Rub-A-Dub Dub"* as you play with three large dolls and a tub. Encourage the baby to touch the dolls.

SENSORY PERCEPTION

While changing the baby, sing or say the *"Rub-A-Dub Dub"* poem.

LANGUAGE SKILLS

Read a book about bath time.

SOCIAL AND EMOTIONAL

Sing: *"Rub-A-Dub Dub"* (Early Childhood Curriculum Resource Book).

LARGE MOTOR SKILLS

Let the baby play in an inch of water. Add "three men" and a "tub" that float in the water.

SMALL MOTOR SKILLS

Fill a pan with several squeeze toys (sponges and a washcloth). Let the baby play with the toys in the pan while you sing, *"Rub-a-Dub Dub."* (Early Childhood Curriculum Resource Book)

SENSORY PERCEPTION

Sing with the babies, *"This is the Way We Wash"* (Early Childhood Curriculum Resource Book). Use a small amount of non-toxic baby soap and water and rub their hands and rinse.

LANGUAGE SKILLS

Read a book about bath time.

SOCIAL AND EMOTIONAL

Sing: *"Rub-A-Dub Dub"* (Early Childhood Curriculum Resource Book).

Watch Me Move

T HEME X

ROLLING

LARGE MOTOR SKILLS

Lay the baby on her back. Hold a small toy above her face. Move the toy to one side, and see if the baby will turn over toward the toy.

SMALL MOTOR SKILLS

Lay the baby on her side on a mat. Watch the baby roll over.

SENSORY PERCEPTION

Shake a rattle and see if the baby will roll over to find the sound.

LANGUAGE SKILLS

Read: *"Roll Over!"* by Merle Peek.

SOCIAL AND EMOTIONAL

Sing: *"Roll, Roll, Roll the Ball"* (Early Childhood Curriculum Resource Book).

LARGE MOTOR SKILLS

Lay the baby on her stomach on a rolled log blanket. Roll the baby back and forth as you sing a song.

SMALL MOTOR SKILLS

Make a ramp for the baby to roll toys down.

SENSORY PERCEPTION

Find different types of toys that will roll. Encourage the baby to roll the toys. Tell the baby what she is doing.

LANGUAGE SKILLS

Encourage the baby to use words. For example, say "Will you roll me the ball?" and, "You rolled the ball to me."

SOCIAL AND EMOTIONAL

Sing: *"Roll, Roll, Roll the Ball"* (Early Childhood Curriculum Resource Book).

TURNING

INFANTS 0-6 MONTHS

LARGE MOTOR SKILLS

Shine a light in the direction the baby is looking. Move the light from side to side so she can turn her head.

SMALL MOTOR SKILLS

Lay the baby on her stomach. Hold on to both sides of the baby, and gently turn the baby over to one side, then to the other side. Say as you turn the baby, "Turn over to your left," and "Turn over to your right."

SENSORY PERCEPTION

Shake a toy. See if the baby turns to see the toy.

LANGUAGE SKILLS

Read: "Baby's First Book," by Tiny Love.

SOCIAL AND EMOTIONAL

Sing: "Wheels on the Bus" (Early Childhood Curriculum Resource Book). Do the movements to the song.

Theme X: Watch Me Move

LARGE MOTOR SKILLS

Put your hands under the baby's feet and move her feet and legs up and down and around, like turning pedals on a bicycle. Encourage the baby to push on your hands.

SMALL MOTOR SKILLS

Give the baby a turning toy. Show her how to turn the toy by herself.

SENSORY PERCEPTION

With the baby, look at her picture books. Talk about what you see and let the baby turn the page by herself. Assist the baby if she needs some help.

LANGUAGE SKILLS

Place a turning toy in the baby's hands. Place your hand over the baby's hand and turn the toy together. Say as you turn, "We are turning the toy."

SOCIAL AND EMOTIONAL

Sing: *"The Wheels on the Bus"* (Early Childhood Curriculum Resource Book).

BALANCING

LARGE MOTOR SKILLS

Hold the baby firmly under her arms. Gently raise the baby up and slowly let the baby down.

SMALL MOTOR SKILLS

Sit the baby on your lap and gently raise the baby up and slowly let the baby down.

SENSORY PERCEPTION

Support the baby on your knees and gently sway or rock the baby back and forth.

LANGUAGE SKILLS

Read a book about balancing.

SOCIAL AND EMOTIONAL

Sing and do: *"Balance On My Knee"* (Early Childhood Curriculum Resource Book).

LARGE MOTOR SKILLS

Support the baby on your knees. Rock gently and help the baby practice balancing herself.

SMALL MOTOR SKILLS

Hold the baby's hands as she walks. This will help her learn to balance herself. See if she can balance herself by holding onto sturdy furniture in the room.

SENSORY PERCEPTION

Balance a block on top of another block to build a tower. Encourage the baby to do the same. Talk about what is happening.

LANGUAGE SKILLS

Read: *"Baby Things"* by Catherine and Laurence Anholt.

SOCIAL AND EMOTIONAL

Sing and do: *"Balance on My Knee"* (Early Childhood Curriculum Resource Book).

HOLDING ON

LARGE MOTOR SKILLS

Hold the baby with her head on your shoulder and walk around the room. See if the baby can balance her own head.

SMALL MOTOR SKILLS

Place a small toy or soft block in the palm of the baby's hand. See if the baby will hold onto the toy.

SENSORY PERCEPTION

Give the baby a rattle. See if the baby will hold onto the rattle.

LANGUAGE SKILLS

Read soft books that the baby can hold.

SOCIAL AND EMOTIONAL

Sing, *"Pat-a-Cake"* (Early Childhood Curriculum Resource Book).

LARGE MOTOR SKILLS

Find a box big enough to hold the baby and some toys. Wind up a music toy and put it into the box with the baby. See how she reacts.

SMALL MOTOR SKILLS

Show the baby how to hold a clothespin to drop it into a can. Encourage the baby to drop the clothespin into the can.

SENSORY PERCEPTION

Give the baby a wind up toy. Encourage the baby to wind up the toy and listen to the sounds it makes.

LANGUAGE SKILLS

Play the game of "Holding On" with the baby. Give the baby a toy. Say, "Hold the block." To develop vocabulary concepts add descriptive words. Repeat the sentence adding different descriptive words. For example: "Hold the red ball."

SOCIAL AND EMOTIONAL

Sing: *"Ring Around the Rosy"* (Early Childhood Curriculum Resource Book). Hold hands as you sing.

THROWING

LARGE MOTOR SKILLS

Take a colorful silk scarf and wave it back and forth over the baby's crib two times. See if she notices.

SMALL MOTOR SKILLS

Swing the mobiles back and forth over the baby's crib. See if she notices.

SENSORY PERCEPTION

Hold the baby up and place her hand on the mobile.

LANGUAGE SKILLS

Talk to the baby describing how the mobiles are swinging.

SOCIAL AND EMOTIONAL

Sing: *"Wave, Wave, Wave the Scarf"* (Early Childhood Curriculum Resource Book).

LARGE MOTOR SKILLS

Give the baby a basket and soft toys she can throw into the basket.

SMALL MOTOR SKILLS

Make a target for outdoor play. Encourage the baby to throw toward the target. For texture, use different balls.

SENSORY PERCEPTION

If the baby is walking, play the throwing game in a standing position. Use and describe different textures and colors.

LANGUAGE SKILLS

Gently toss a sock ball so that it bounces before reaching the baby. Tell the baby to throw the ball back to you. Say, "Good throw. Now I'll throw the ball back to you."

SOCIAL AND EMOTIONAL

Sing: *"Throw, Throw, Throw the Ball,"* (Early Childhood Curriculum Resource Book).

Bibliography

Anholt, Catherine and Laurence. *"Baby's Things."* New York, New York: Baby Publishing Company, 1991.

Badger, Earladeen. *"Infant/Toddler: Introducing Your Child to the Joy of Learning."* New York, New York: Instructo/McGraw Hill, Inc., 1981.

Bowrlant, Beth, et al. *"Active Learning for Infants."* Menlo Park, NY: Addison-Wesley Publishing Company, 1987.

Bredekemp, Sue and Carol Copple, ed. *"Developmentally Appropriate Practice in Early Programs. "* Washington D.C., 1997.

Cherrington, Janelle. *"What's That Smell?"* New York, New York: Simon and Schuster Children's Publishing, 1999.

Cocca-Leffler, Maryann. *"Mommy Hugs."* New York, New York: Simon and Schuster Children's Publishing, 1997.

Cocca-Leffler, Maryann. *"Daddy Hugs."* New York, New York: Simon and Schuster Children's Publishing, 1997.

Colker Laura J. and Dianne Trister Dodge. *"The Creative Learning Curriculum for Early Childhood."* Washington, D.C.: Teaching Strategies, Inc., 1992.

Cowles, Milly, Ph.D *"Where Have all the Data Gone?"* Washington, D.C.: National Association for the Education of Young Children, (2001): 23-26.

Davis, Allison. *"Best Friends."* New York, New York: Random House Children's Publishing, 1992.

Dobbs, Siobhan. *"Ting-a-Lings!"* New York, New York: DK Publishing, Inc., 1999.

Elkind, David. *"What Makes Young Children Laugh?"* (Child Care Information Exchange.) New Richmond, WI: St. Croix Press, 2000.

Ellis, Sue. *"Baby Things Up and Under."* New York: 4 Learning. New York, 2003.

"Finger Frolics" compiled by Liz Cromwell, Dixie Cromwell, and John R. Faitel; Contributing authors: Rebecca Baynton, Colleen Kobe, Lois Peters, and unknown. Livonia, Michigan: Partner Press, 1976.

Frankel, Valerie. *"How to Talk to Your Child."* Parenting (2002): 92-95.

Guthrie, Woody. *"Nursery Days, Put Your Finger In The Air."* Washington, DC: Smithsonian Folkways, 1992.

Hanks, Betty. *"Early Childhood Curriculum Resource Guide, Infants 0-12 Months."* Bryan, Texas: Life Long Learning, 2003.

Holley, Cynthia and Faraday Burditt. *"Resources for Every Day in Every Way."* Carthage, Illinois: Fearon Teacher Aids, 1989.

Love, Tiny. *"Baby's First Book."* New York, New York: Genius Babies, Incorporated, 1998.

Munsch, Robert. *"Love You Forever."* Scarborough, Ontario: Firefly Books, 1986.

Parr, Todd. *"Funny Faces."* Boston, Massachusetts: Little Brown and Company, 2002.

Patrick, Denise Lewis. *"What Does Baby See?"* Racine, Washington: West Publishing Company, 1990.

Peek, Merle. *"Roll Over!"* Boston, Massachusetts: Houghton Mifflin Company Publishing, 1991.

Sanders, Stephen W. *"Active Learning for Life."* Washington, D.C.: National Association for the Education of Young Children, 2002.

Shea, Jan Fisher. *"No Board Babies."* Seattle, Washington: Bear Creek Publications, 1986.

Silberg, Jackie. *"Games to Play with Babies."* Mt. Rainer, Maryland: Gryphon House, 1993.

Szamreta, Joanne M. *"Peekaboo Power."* Washington, D.C.: Young Children (2002): 88-96.

Warren, Jean, Ed. *"Piggyback songs."* Everett, WA: Warren Publishing House, 1981.

Wojtowycz, David. *"Eat Up Dudley."* New York, New York: Watt Publishing Group, March 2002.

Notes

Notes

Notes